BEGINNER'S GUIDE TO
CYANOTYPE

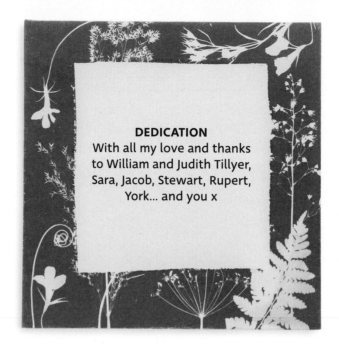

DEDICATION
With all my love and thanks
to William and Judith Tillyer,
Sara, Jacob, Stewart, Rupert,
York… and you x

First published in 2024
Search Press Limited
Wellwood, North Farm Road,
Tunbridge Wells, Kent TN2 3DR

Text, diagrams and templates copyright
© Kim Tillyer, 2024

For photographs on pages 9, 11, 22 (T) and 23 (T+M),
please refer to page 110 for copyright information.

Photographs on pages 3, 23 (B), 24–25, 33 (TR), 34 (B), 42,
43, 45, 47, 49, 51, 53, 57, 61, 63, 64, 65, 67, 71, 73, 77, 79, 85, 87,
91, 93 and 97: Stacy Grant, www.stacygrant.co.uk
Copyright © Search Press Ltd.

All remaining photographs:
Mark Davison, www.markdavison.com
Copyright © Search Press Ltd

Design copyright © Search Press Ltd. 2024

ISBN: 978-1-80092-095-8
ebook ISBN: 978-1-80093-086-5

SUPPLIERS
If you have difficulty in obtaining any of the materials and
equipment mentioned in this book, then please visit the
Search Press website for details of suppliers:
www.searchpress.com

DOWNLOADABLE TEMPLATES
Extra copies of the templates are also available to
download free from the Bookmarked Hub. Search for
this book by title or ISBN: the files can be found under
'Book Extras'. Membership of the Bookmarked online
community is free: www.bookmarkedhub.com

ABOUT THE AUTHOR
For more information about Kim Tillyer and her work,
please visit:
☼ her website, www.witchmountain.co.uk
☼ her Instagram page, via @witchmountain
☼ her Facebook page, via @witchmountainart

MIX
Paper | Supporting
responsible forestry
FSC® C016973

BEGINNER'S GUIDE TO
CYANOTYPE

Beautiful projects to print with light

KIM TILLYER

SEARCH PRESS

CONTENTS

INTRODUCTION

I have my artist parents to thank for introducing me to the blue magic that is cyanotype printing.

At some point in the late 1970s, probably in the long summer holidays, my brother and I were given a pack of Sunprint paper and sent off into the garden to experiment. The paper we played with was pre-coated with something mysteriously light-sensitive, which turned blue in the sunlight, and left an impression of whatever was placed on the surface. Once the paper was rinsed in water, this impression was fixed and more or less permanent.

I loved it – the unpredictablility, and the building excitement as the water revealed the image. But because the paper was small and thin, and relatively expensive back then, it remained a novelty, something fun to do with kids on a sunny day.

Many, many years later, I was a 'mature' student studying for a degree in Textiles and Surface Design and looking for different techniques to create interesting sketchbook imagery. I remembered that someone (probably my brother, since he had become a photographer by then) had bought my children a pack of the same paper. I dusted it off and started my blue-and-white adventures once again.

It wasn't until I'd left university, and no longer had access to all the other printing facilities there, that I started to look at ways I could print at home. I turned to cyanotype again, and I began to investigate printing fabric and paper with the technique. As a child, I'd never even thought about what the magic coating was on the Sunprint paper I'd used, so it was wonderful to discover just how easy it was to mix the solution myself and achieve exciting results on all sorts of surfaces (some unintentional, like the kitchen table!).

Much of my artwork now involves making cyanotype prints, on both paper and fabric. I layer my drawings or photographs with plants and found objects, and often I add embroidery stitches to create ethereal, illustrative pieces.

I hope this book will inspire you to have fun experimenting with cyanotype. I know you will enjoy discovering how to use it: cyanotype is a hand-made process with countless creative and educational possibilities that can be used by anyone – not just photographers, artists, illustrators and educators – to achieve satisfying results from the very beginning.

Folding
notebook idea

The longer an image is
left to develop, the more
detail is revealed –
from plain silhouettes
to veined petals.

What is CYANOTYPE?

Essentially, cyanotype printing is a way of producing images using UV light (often from the sun) to oxidize a light-sensitive emulsion, made by mixing two chemicals with water.

Cyanotype printing developed alongside early photography. It is often described as an 'alternative process' (an untraditional or non-commercial photographic printing process), along with carbon printing, wet-plate collodions, pinhole photography, daguerreotypes and many more.

Cyanotype's appeal lies in its simplicity and accessibility, but most obviously in the glorious shade of blue that occurs when Potassium Ferricyanide and Ferric Ammonium Citrate are combined and bathed in sunlight – Prussian blue.

The colour blue

Studies have consistently shown that, of all the colours, blue – in all its hues – is the most popular. Blue has a calming effect on the mind, evoking cloudless skies, clear waters and distant hills as well as having associations with spirituality and contemplation. There is something about the combination of blue and white in design that is timeless – think of Chinese blue-and-white porcelain, Delftware and Cornishware™ – and goes some way in explaining the enduring popularity of cyanotype. (See Endnotes, page 110.)

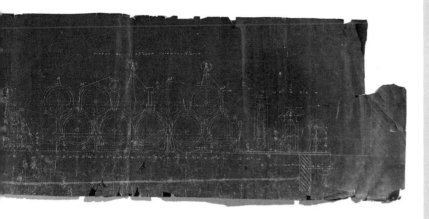

History and uses

The process was invented in 1842 by polymath Sir John Herschel (1792–1871) as a way of easily making accurate copies of his prolific technical notes and diagrams. Herschel was the nephew of a remarkable woman, astronomer Caroline Herschel, and was himself an astronomer. He was also a mathematician and chemist, and his writings influenced the naturalist Charles Darwin (their tombs lie side by side in Westminster Abbey, London, UK). Herschel contributed to the improvement of early photography by sharing his discoveries with Fox Talbot (who invented salt printing and calotype photography) and Louis Daguerre (who went on to develop daguerreotype photography). The copies of notes and diagrams that Herschel made were called 'blueprints', and we still use the word today to describe ideas, plans and technical drawings, even though the method was eventually replaced in the 1940s with the newer, cheaper copying technique of diazo printing, which produces 'whiteprints' (dark blue lines on a white background), and later still by Xerography and then modern digital printing.

Cyanotype as a creative and aesthetic process was really championed by a friend and associate of Herschel and Talbot, Anna Atkins (1799–1871). Unlike many girls of her time, Atkins had an unusually scientific education, encouraged by her father John George Children – a renowned chemist and zoologist, and a Fellow of the Royal Entomological Society. Atkins was an illustrator, writer and botanist, and in her desire to update William Harvey's *Manual of British Algae* (1841) she combined Herschel's blueprints with Talbot's 'photogenic drawings' and created what is now considered the world's first photographically illustrated book: *Photographs of British Algae: Cyanotype Impressions* (1845–1853). Each copy was a work of art, individually bound and printed; it even included handwritten text, printed by writing on paper that had been oiled to make it transparent.

'The difficulty of making accurate drawings of objects as minute as many of the Algae and Confera has induced me to avail myself of Sir John Herschel's beautiful process of Cyanotype, to obtain impressions of the plants themselves, which I have much pleasure in offering to my botanical friends.'

– Excerpt from Anna Atkins' introduction to *Photographs of British Algae: Cyanotype Impressions* (1845–1853); see also the top-right image, opposite.

(See Endnotes, page 110.)

Women's work in science and discovery has often been overlooked. Despite the Victorian passion for natural history that saw fern fever ('pteridomania'), and a craze for collecting and pressing seaweed, women were barred from membership of the Royal Society and the Linnaean Society. (It's possible Linnaeus' controversial system of classifying plant parts as 'male' or 'female' made the society seem a little risqué!) It is only fairly recently that Atkins' work and contribution to both science and art has been celebrated and truly valued. On 16 March 2015, the day's 'Google Doodle' was a cyanotype image in celebration of Atkins' 216th birthday.

Atkins' representations of seaweed, algae, flowers and ferns (in collaboration with her close friend, Anne Dixon) are still the archetypal images that most people think of when they imagine cyanotypes, and even now they are some of the most striking, beautiful and technically perfect examples.

In the following centuries, as technology advanced, people became interested again in hand-made photographic processes alongside – and in contrast to – modern digital photography. Artists began experimenting with cyanotype image transfer onto other porous substrates such as ceramic bisque (unglazed pottery), natural fabrics, wood and gelatine-coated glass – and the results don't even have to be blue! It's possible to tone cyanotype prints with plant tannins after bleaching them using common household detergents.

In around 2008, when I first started making cyanotype prints, there was very little easily available information and hardly any books; now, the materials and equipment you need to get started are much more easily accessible and, thanks to the internet, the technique has gradually regained the attention it deserves. Social media has made the process more popular too: hashtags and interest groups have been created so ideas, images and new techniques (like the experimental method of #wetcyan) can be shared, and there's even World Cyanotype Day (celebrated annually on the last Saturday in September).

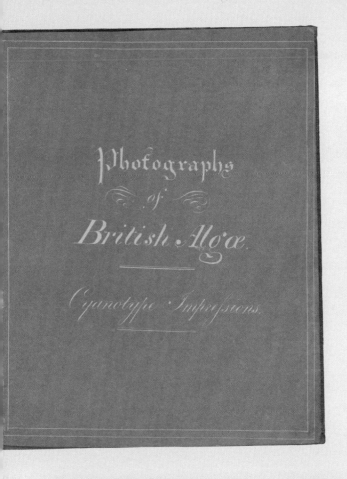

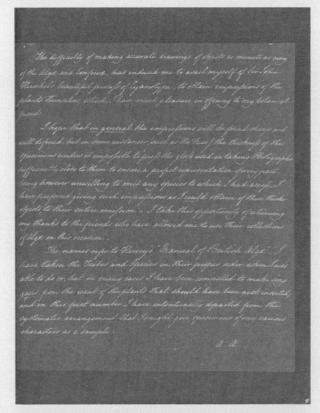

Rhodomenia laciniata.

Ptilota serices.

Tools and
MATERIALS

The beauty of cyanotype is that you really need very little to get started, and it's perfectly possible to do all of the projects in this book on your kitchen table, in the garden or even in the park or on the beach. Many of the things you might need are probably already in your cupboards (and those that aren't are widely available online), and you won't need a darkroom or expensive equipment. Just clear a space, gather everything you need and have fun.

Stage 1 necessities:
For measuring, mixing, storing, applying and processing

- ☼ Two chemicals – **Ferric Ammonium Citrate** (a fine greenish-yellow powder with the consistency of icing sugar) and **Potassium Ferricyanide** (a gritty red powder with the consistency of caster sugar). There are also pre-mixed solutions commercially available, as well as measured kits, but it's really simple to mix your own and you can even experiment with the ratios as you become more confident.

- ☼ **Measuring spoons** (a teaspoon, a half teaspoon and a third of a teaspoon), **measuring jugs** and **tools to stir with** (I use craft sticks).

- ☼ **Light-proof jars** for mixing and storing. They should be opaque or made from amber glass, if possible, to protect the solution from UV light. I've found that the ideal containers are those opaque, black plastic pots from cosmetic companies, but if you don't want to wait until you've used up all your moisturizer you can buy light-proof containers from specialist photography suppliers.

- ☼ **Water**. I've always used tap water with no problems, but if you live in an area with extremely high alkaline levels/hard water, it might be worth you using filtered or distilled water for a more neutral pH.

- ☼ **Brushes**, for painting the solution onto the surface. Foam brushes are lovely for giving an even coverage but Japanese hake brushes are my favourite.

- ☼ **Surface for 'printing'.** You can be more adventurous later, but I recommend starting with paper. Make sure it's strong enough to stand up to soaking and rinsing. If you're keen to use fabrics, stick to natural fabrics such as cotton, linen and silk.

- ☼ **Somewhere dark to dry the coated surface**. I use an empty drawer or cupboard shelf. A reusable black plastic sheet (an opaque bin liner would work well) is useful to cover your papers as they dry if your workspace is particularly bright.

- ☼ **Reusable protective cover**, such as a plastic sheet, newsprint or other clean-waste paper to protect your working surface – especially if you're using your kitchen table!

- ☼ **Emergency cleaning cloth**, for spillages.

- ☼ **Nitrile gloves, goggles and a face mask** (see the note on health and safety on page 16).

- ☼ Optional: **digital scales**, for accurate measuring.

- ☼ Optional: **Litmus paper**, for testing your water's pH.

Working in the dark

Note that you can work under a normal electric light, so consider coating and drying surfaces at night if your space is especially bright. Don't forget to store things in the dark until you are ready to print.

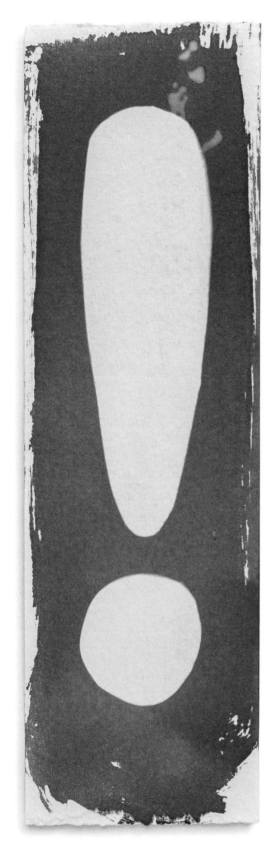

Health, safety and environmental concerns

The two chemicals used in the stage 1 process are iron salts, and because of this neither of the chemicals (despite the 'cyanide' bit in 'Potassium Ferricyanide') are dangerous when used properly. In fact, Ferric Ammonium Citrate (FAC) is sometimes called E381 and is used in the production of the famous Scottish carbonated drink Irn Bru (admittedly in tiny quantities – 0.002% apparently); it also has some medical applications.

That said, please do not drink, inhale or allow prolonged skin contact with either the powder or solution! The chemicals are classed as 'Hazardous/Mild Irritant', so it's a good idea to wear a face mask and goggles while measuring and mixing (FAC is a fine powder that could easily be inhaled). Wear nitrile gloves during the rinsing part – especially if you have sensitive skin.

Store the chemicals in a cool dry place away from light and in air-tight containers (FAC tends to clump and solidify if allowed to absorb moisture from the atmosphere), and keep them away from food preparation areas, inquisitive pets and small children. Do not use the same utensils for cooking! Very dilute chemicals are safe to pour down the sink or onto ornamental garden borders, but do not dispose of undiluted chemicals in domestic refuse or drains. Mike Ware, a scientist and leading expert on the cyanotype process, has written in more detail about this in section 7 of his essay 'Cyanomicon – History, Science and Art of Cyanotype: photographic printing in Prussian blue' (see Further Reading on page 109); this is available as a free downloadable PDF in English, and is worth a read if (as we all should be) you are concerned about environmental impact and best practice to minimize potential damage.

Finally, it is worth noting that Potassium Ferricyanide can, if mixed with strong acids, release the highly toxic gas Hydrogen Cyanide. Please don't worry about this: it is not going to occur during any of your printmaking because you will be following the recipe, but it's worth pointing out that care should always be taken to follow instructions when using, mixing, storing and disposing of chemicals.

Stage 2 necessities:
For designing, developing and rinsing

☀ Things to lay on the paper to make a print. We'll call these '**design elements**' – more on this later!

☀ A **flat, portable surface**, such as a board, sketchbook or large piece of stiff cardboard, for easily carrying your work to the light source.

☀ **Sheet of glass or transparent acrylic** (such as Perspex®) to lay over your design elements to hold them close to the paper, stopping them blowing away. Glass from an old picture frame and some bulldog clips would work well, or a purpose-made photographic contact print frame if you're lucky enough to have one. Some glass blocks UV light, so make sure yours is just plain glass. If I'm using glass, I also like to wrap the edges with masking tape to protect my fingers from the sharp edges.

☀ **A light source**. Sunlight is the most obvious choice! However, if you want to process indoors or on a grey day, UV lightbulbs can be used in purpose-made or DIY exposure units to recreate sunlight. (LED blacklights with a 365nm wavelength, such as Everbeam, or the ones commonly used in insect traps such as Wemlite BL368, are the ones in my lamps.) Using a light unit will also make it easier to get consistent results: you will have a constant and predictable light that you can accurately time – unlike the typically changeable Lake District weather that I have!

☀ **Access to water**. Prints need lots of rinsing and, depending on the paper, a prolonged soak. In addition to the kitchen sink, I've found that plastic cat litter trays (transparent, white or cream, so that you can tell what colour the water is) or large washing-up bowls are perfect and much cheaper than the special photographic developing trays.

☀ **Somewhere to hang your work, to dry** – this can be a washing line with pegs; a print-drying rack, if you have one; or you could simply lay your work flat on clean newsprint or blotting paper.

☀ **Timing device** (watch, clock on smartphone, kitchen timer, etc.).

☀ Optional: **tongs**, to use when rinsing your printed paper or fabric.

☀ Optional: **distilled white vinegar or citric acid**. This is not vital but a few drops in the initial rinse helps acidify the water and brighten the print, particularly of you live in an area with water that is very alkaline.

Printing surfaces

Any surface that the solution will stick to, and that can withstand the washing process without falling apart, can be used for making cyanotype prints – even empty teabags! It's fun to experiment and, like any other media, the results will vary slightly according to the qualities of the surface you choose.

Printing on paper

If you are using paper, the most important thing to be aware of is that cyanotypes are acid loving and really can't stand an alkaline environment – i.e. a pH over 7.5. Because some papers are 'buffered' to reduce the acidity for archival purposes, this can affect the print and its durability. Therefore, specialist paper (such as Hahnemühle Platinum Rag) is often recommended and can be bought from photographic and art suppliers.

However, please don't be afraid to try whatever you have handy. I've found that Khadi paper (a widely available cotton rag in various sizes and weights), most watercolour papers (I use ARCHES) and good-quality cartridge papers (over about 150gsm/40lbs) work well; and I've also had unexpectedly lovely results on mountboard off-cuts, tea-bag paper, fragile Japanese woodblock paper and even paper doilies.

There have been some very detailed studies made by cyanotype practitioners on the different results achieved on various papers, which are definitely worth studying, but for me the beauty of an analogue process is the unpredictablility and element of surprise. So, if there's a paper or another printing surface you'd like to try then give it a go – you have nothing to lose.

Printing on fabric

Printing on fabric is what first interested me in cyanotype, and I have to acknowledge that everything I know today started with a small kit and a book by Ruth Brown, a textile artist and bookbinder from East Yorkshire, UK.

CHOOSING YOUR FABRIC

The fabric used must be 'natural'– in other words, made from plant or animal fibres rather than man-made materials such as polyester. I've also found that fabric, unlike paper, has to be fully dried after coating, and needs a slightly longer exposure time too, for the best results.

Some fabric suppliers provide large samples of a variety of natural printing and dyeing fabrics (shown opposite and on page 22), and it's a good idea to test a selection of fibres so that you discover the one that gives you your favourite result. All of the samples were exposed for exactly the same amount of time, but the resulting shade of blue and crispness of image for each one is quite different.

A lot of the fabric I use is 'loomstate', which means it has not been bleached or undergone any treatments since leaving the loom, making it easier to 'dye' with cyanotype. This also means the fibres sometimes contain natural flecks and weird imperfections that can affect the print – although 'perfection' can be overrated, as Leonard Cohen and the makers of Persian carpets knew. Embrace the unpredictable; it's what makes the work unique.

Testing a range of fabrics for this book gave me a better understanding of how each one reacts, including individual drying times. For example, I realized I could have made life a lot easier for myself in the past if I'd used mediumweight cotton or poplin for a particular work, as I would have had a crisp, bright print and it would have dried much more quickly – so it had less time to discolour before printing.

If you're not sure which fabric to use, calico is a really good choice for all these projects and is cheap enough that you can afford not to be too heartbroken if things don't work out. When you feel you've cracked the process, imagine what you can make with bamboo silk or rich cotton velvet!

'Blue, darkly, deeply, beautifully blue.'

– Robert Southey (1774–1843), Poet Laureate.

cambridge natural

denim white

cotton linen mix

printer's mediumweight natural

batiste

mulberry silk

poplin

bamboo silk

linen

cotton velvet

calico loomstate

PREPARING AND CARING FOR YOUR FABRIC

Often fabric – even one designed for printing or dyeing – has protective coatings and other finishes that can lead to unpredictable results. So, even with a commercial craft blank, it's good practice to wash, dry and iron your material before coating it.

Cyanotype textiles are sometimes confused with indigo dyeing, as both result in gorgeous shades of blue. However, you can usually tell the difference by checking the reverse of the fabric: dyed textiles have colour on both sides but, like many print methods, cyanotype is applied to one side of the surface and therefore will only show on one side of the fabric, even if the fabric is very thin.

One thing to consider is the purpose of the item to which you're applying your cyanotype solution. Although the print is fairly robust, it can be damaged by abrasion and agitation during frequent washing or ironing. I would not recommend putting anything printed with cyanotype in the washing machine.

This is why cyanotype possibly wouldn't be the best choice for printing a tea towel, for example. The most important thing to remember when it comes to washing your cyanotype textiles is that alkaline is its enemy, so don't use any washing detergent that contains phosphates, bleach or sodium. Handwashing using a tiny drop of eco- and animal-friendly washing-up liquid (dish soap) seems to work for me, but test on an inconspicuous area or sample print before you risk your beautiful final piece. You definitely can't just chuck your carefully printed T-shirt in with the rest of your washing – not because it will dye everything blue (cyanotype will not 'run' in the wash), but because it will come out faded and sad.

Beyond paper and fabric: other surfaces

A quick glance at the internet will reveal a whole world of unusual and innovative ways that artists and photographers have used cyanotype to experiment with printing on a variety of surfaces and objects. If you can get the light-sensitive solution to stick, it is theoretically possible to print on anything. This is the case especially with organic surfaces – from wood, clay and pebbles to egg shells and even apple cores (as in Manuel Limay Incil's work, top right – see Endnotes, page 110).

Experimental artists have also taken advantage of cyanotype's versatility to perfect the process of printing onto glass and ceramics. Jo Howell is one such artist, and has used a gelatine primer and a 1:1 recipe, with beautiful and ethereal results (see the middle-right image). Printing on glass almost takes the technique full circle, back to the glass plate negatives used by the earliest photographers. This is definitely not my area of expertise, and I highly recommend Jo's website for further reading if you've got the blueprint bug and want to dive deeper (see Endnotes, page 110).

I found that a lot of my results where I'd experimented with other surfaces were wildly unpredictable, and a bit frustrating to start with. Yet, as Jo says, 'I have continued to revisit the process in more recent projects, to varying degrees of success. Sometimes, it is my own fault for being impatient or hurrying the process when I know fine well that patience goes a long way when you are working with the blues'.

As this book is a beginner's guide, the only 'unusual surface' I've used in this book is air-dry clay (see the bottom-right image). I wanted to create a simple project that would almost certainly work for you and give you confidence to explore further, because there are SO many creative possibilities.

Basic
TECHNIQUES

To demonstrate the key stages in making a cyanotype print, we'll be making a simple project that will involve little effort but will leave you with a lovely bookmark keepsake or gift. We'll also take a look at how the solution changes depending on the amount of exposure to light: you will see that the longer it is left in the sunlight, the deeper the shade of blue.

You will need:

- ☼ Necessities on pages 14–23
- ☼ Thick paper or card – I like to use heavyweight watercolour paper or left-over pieces of mountboard
- ☼ A piece of card big enough to cover your bookmark completely
- ☼ Chosen design element(s) – I'm using a feather
- ☼ Ribbon, scissors, craft knife and a hole punch

Design elements

There are two main groups of design elements – things you lay on the paper to make a 'photogram', and photographic or hand-drawn negatives on acetate, which we'll talk about in detail later.

Because anything that casts a shadow will create an image, with the photogram technique you're limited only by the size of the paper and your imagination. Design elements don't have to be perfect fern fronds or pressed flowers; sometimes, the most ordinary object makes the most satisfying and unusual print. For example, at one workshop, one of my students used spirals of wood shavings left after previous course on longbow making!

Look around your house and you will find all sorts of interesting shapes to experiment with, from cutlery to pens and scissors. I've seen really interesting prints made using scattered elastic bands, beach pebbles, laddered tights and even a frozen spider's web!

For crisp, clear prints, flat objects that can be held in close contact with the printing surface using a sheet of glass or transparent acrylic work. However, 3D objects are exciting to print too. Think of a cookie cutter – the outline will be crisp and white as it's in full contact with the surface of the paper, while the sides will print as a ghostly shadow (depending on the direction of the light) that seems to be almost lifting off the page.

Here are some examples of simple objects you can use as your design elements.

☼ Plants and leaves, especially tiny, often over-looked things such as the blue speedwell you might find in a lawn (this has lovely heart-shaped seed pods). Experiment with grasses, dandelion clocks, autumn leaves and sycamore keys.

☼ Door keys, hair grips, buttons and pieces of jewellery.

☼ Feathers.

☼ Lace and other open-weave fabrics, such as scrim or hessian/jute/burlap.

☼ Bubble wrap, the netting some fruit comes in and see-through plastic packaging.

☼ Nuts and bolts and old bike or watch parts.

☼ Paintbrushes, scissors, cutlery.

☼ Your own hands and feet.

☼ Lentils, pasta shapes, confetti, pebbles and sand.

Fun fact: giant cyanotype

In September 2017, in Thessaloniki, Greece, a photographer called Stefanos Tsakiris got people to lie down on a very large piece of pre-coated fabric to create a record-breaking 276.64m² (2977.72 ft²) 'gyanotype' (giant cyanotype).

Stage 1:
Measuring, mixing, storing, applying and processing

I: MEASURING, MIXING AND STORING

I use the same recipe for all my work. It's not hard to remember and can easily be adjusted to make a larger quantity. Some people use digital scales to be super-accurate with measurements, to get very consistent results, but I've found that this recipe is pretty forgiving and teaspoon measures work fine for me.

Make sure you have an opaque bottle in which to store your solution, especially if you're not going to use it all at once. Remember to store any left-over solution in a dark place. Depending on how well it's stored, technically it should keep for a few days up to three weeks. However, the solution will work for as long as it remains yellow/pale green – I've seen great results from year-old solution found in the back of a print studio cupboard!

You can use a pre-mixed solution if you wish, purchased from a photography or art supplier; in which case, follow the manufacturer's instructions carefully.

1 To make 50ml (¼ cup) of processing solution (this should be enough to coat plenty of paper or fabric, and is roughly the volume used for each of the projects in this book), add 6.25g (1⅓ tsps) of Ferric Ammonium Citrate to a jar and mix with 25ml (5 tsps) of water with a spoon until it's completely dissolved.

2 In a separate jar, add 2.5g (½ tsp) of Potassium Ferricyanide and mix with 25ml (5 tsps) of water until the powder has dissolved.

3 You now have two jars of solution that will become light-sensitive when you combine them. Carefully pour the two into an opaque, light-proof bottle (I'm using a clear glass jar so you can see what the combined solution looks like) and then mix them together, making sure all the crystals have dissolved. The liquid is now sensitive to light and ready to use for coating your paper and fabric.

4 Now bookmark this recipe page, so it's always easy to find!

II: APPLYING AND PROCESSING

1 Choose somewhere with low light to lay out your paper. It doesn't have to be pitch dark, and you won't need a darkroom with a red bulb; you could simply close curtains or blinds, or work at night under normal household lightbulbs, and neither will affect the solution. Cover your workspace with a reusable protective cover to absorb inevitable drips. Remember to clean up spillages quickly – at one of the venues where I teach, someone must have been over-enthusiastic when coating the paper, and it wasn't noticed until the floor turned blue a few days later!

2 Apply a very thin, even layer of solution to your paper using your chosen brush. Try to avoid overloading your brush or over-wetting the paper so that it doesn't drip or pool on the surface. Remember you can use the solution like paint, so don't feel you have to coat the whole surface or have straight edges – brush marks are lovely and add a beautiful hand-made quality.

3 Lay your coated papers in a dark space to dry – often I use a drawer lined with newsprint or cover them on a shelf, but you could use a proper print-drying rack covered in a black plastic sheet.

4 While the paper dries, clean up and gather everything you need for the next stage.

Stage 2:
Designing, developing, rinsing and drying

This is the fun bit!

Your dried paper should still be a pale yellow, perhaps very pale green depending on the brand and on certain papers. It's a good idea to keep these face down in a dark place, cover them with a black plastic sheet or store them in an opaque bin liner, to prevent light getting to them: remember they are light-sensitive now and will start to react to any level of UV light, even on a dull day.

I: DESIGNING AND DEVELOPING

1 Place your coated printing surface onto your flat portable surface, the coated side facing up. Arrange your design element(s) over the coated side of your printing surface. Work in a low light if possible and fairly quickly too, especially if it's a bright sunny day. Remember that anything that casts a shadow will make a pale image, and anywhere exposed to light will begin to turn blue.

2 Before making your first print, you may wish to make a 'sandwich': place a sheet of acrylic or glass over the printing surface with the arranged design. The acrylic or glass isn't essential, but it ensures that the design elements have closer contact with the paper and stops things blowing away if you're working outside.

3 Temporarily cover your 'sandwich' while you take it to your light source, then remove the cover once the 'sandwich' is under a UV lamp or in direct sunlight, to begin the exposure.

4 Under a UV lamp (**4a**) or on a dull day outside, coated surfaces will change a little more slowly, so allow at least 15 to 20 minutes under the lamp, up to 30 minutes. On a sunny day in summer, you will immediately see the paper start to change colour as the solution oxidizes (**4b**). Working outside, in full sunshine, everything happens very fast so your print may need only around 15 to 20 minutes of exposure. After a while, you will be able to recognize by eye when a print is ready. Experimenting is all part of the process.

Although UV lamps are great, I always feel sunlight gives more satisfying results. This is very unscientific, but I like to think of the sun as 'full-fat milk' while UV lamps are 'semi-skimmed milk': sunlight gives you full-spectrum' light, not just the one wavelength you have with UV lamps.

Whether under sunshine or UV lamp, the paper will eventually change colour (**4c** and **4d**) and darken to a dusty grey blue, or even light brown – this colour change is the critical thing to look out for and means it is now time to rinse the print to permanently fix it.

Timing your exposure

You can find really useful apps and tools online that help calculate the time needed to expose a print outside, depending on your location, the time of year and weather conditions. As I'm based in the UK, I use the one at www.cyanotype.co.uk

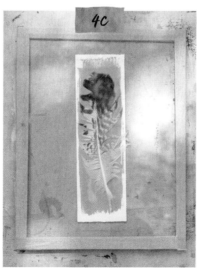

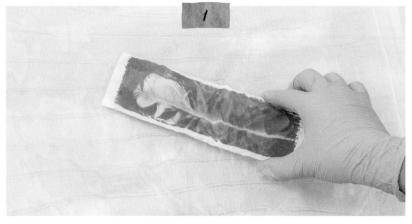

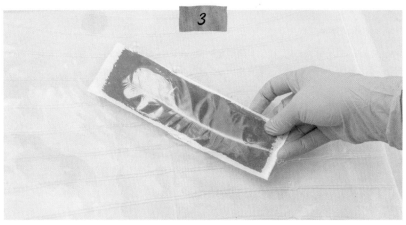

II: RINSING AND DRYING

1 To fix your image, and stop it from processing further, begin by placing the print in a tray of clean cold water and swish it about, making sure there are no air bubbles. This is where you might want to wear gloves, especially if you have sensitive skin, as the solution mixed into the water can irritate and dry out your skin with prolonged contact. Alternatively, or in addition, you could use an old pair of tongs – make sure these aren't used for food preparation.

2 The water will turn yellow as the solution washes out, and your dusty grey paper will be revealed as blue with yellow/white highlights.

3 Keep changing the water and rinsing under the tap until it looks as though all the yellow has gone, then leave your print to soak for five minutes or so more, before rinsing again; this is to ensure that even the solution which has been drawn deep into the fibres of the paper washes away.

4 Finally, hang your work to dry. At this point your work will continue to sharpen and darken, as oxygen completes the developing process, into the final shades of blue and white.

Experimenting

Playing with exposure

As your bookmarks are small designs, take the opportunity to explore exposure times. This exercise will help you to get an idea of how the colour of the coated surface changes according to the time it's exposed and the brightness of the light. Essentially, the longer your work is left in the sunlight, the deeper the shade of blue until it reaches what is termed 'maximum density' or 'D-max' (the darkest possible shade).

1 Follow the steps on pages 28–32, covering your bookmark with a piece of card.

2 Once your 'sandwich' is under the light source (ideally a bright sunny day), move the card down by 1cm (⅜in), revealing the top of the coated paper strip (**2a**). Wait for about a minute before carefully moving it down another 1cm (⅜in) – see **2b**. Repeat this all the way down the bookmark, until all the paper is revealed (**2c**).

3 Follow the rinsing process as detailed opposite.

In the finished photograph, right, you can see that there is an ombré effect with stepped shades of blue, ranging from really dark blue, where it has been in the light longest, to almost white, where the last step was revealed. You could experiment with longer or shorter intervals, but remember that if you're outside the light levels constantly change throughout the day.

Wet cyanotype

By sprinkling water or spooning washing-up liquid (dish soap) bubbles onto a dried or slightly damp coated surface (**1**), then giving the work a long exposure time (around 25–30 minutes), you can make interesting marks and colourations in your cyanotype (**2**).

This is because the water sprinkles or washing-up (dish-soap) bubbles 'corrupt' the solution and alter the developing process. 'Messing' with the process, adding things such as turmeric or vinegar to the water (especially when using plant matter), teamed with a long exposure, leads to all sorts of unexpected shades and effects. Wet cyanotype has become really popular and many artists specialize in this.

HEALTH AND SAFETY WARNING: Please remember any additions should be made to the coated surface, not to the solution itself. Never add anything other than water to the chemicals when they're still powders!

34

Some wet cyanotype techniques: washing-up liquid (dish soap) bubbles and splashes of water. In the top sample, I also diluted some sodium carbonate (washing soda) and painted with it; as sodium carbonate is highly alkaline it acts as a bleach when painted over a dried print, which fades the blue (see page 40).

Sepia toning

Prints don't have to be blue: you can turn your images sepia, like a vintage photograph, using strong tea, coffee or even wine! This is achieved by making use of the tannins naturally found in these substances.

There are endless possibilities to explore with the sepia process – lots of plants, including acorns, alder cones, willow bark and walnut shells, contain tannin and could make different tones.

1 Re-soak a dried and developed print in a weak sodium carbonate (washing soda) solution – 5g (roughly 1 tsp) of sodium carbonate dissolved in 1L (4¼ cups) of water.

2 Wait for the print to fade before rinsing again to remove the soda residue.

3 Now soak your bleached print in a bath of your chosen tannin 'dye', perhaps made with very strong black tea or walnut shells boiled in water and left to cool. You can buy pre-made tannin mixtures from specialist shops selling cyanotype materials. The amount of time you leave your print to soak is up to you, and the depth of sepia tone will depend on how long it is left in the solution.

4 Give your print a final rinse and hang to dry.

LEFT

Natural and hand-drawn design elements printed on the fabric via the traditional method, then toned with tea after bleaching with sodium carbonate (washing soda).

RIGHT

Natural and hand-drawn design elements printed with the traditional method.

A note on experimenting with toning cyanotypes

Toning cyanotypes is becoming hugely popular as a specialism all of its own, and is definitely something I've enjoyed experimenting with for this book. My favourite method was using a handful of alder cones, picked up on a walk, which were boiled to make a tannin dye bath.

You can buy tannin (or tannic acid) specially for toning prints and also try other concoctions such as coffee, red wine, walnut shells, oak bark or even carrots and sweet potato peel!

I keep saying that cyanotype is an experimental process, and even more so when you bring toning into it. For example, every brand of teabag will be slightly different, and the colour achieved will depend on the amount of time the print is left in the dye bath. This means that the result is entirely up to you. It's not even essential to bleach the print first: some nice multi-hued effects can come from toning slightly under-exposed prints, and skipping the bleaching stage.

Toned prints will dry darker and have a vintage, velvety matt quality that can be enhanced on paper with a coat of varnish, such as cold wax medium (I use the one by Gamblin).

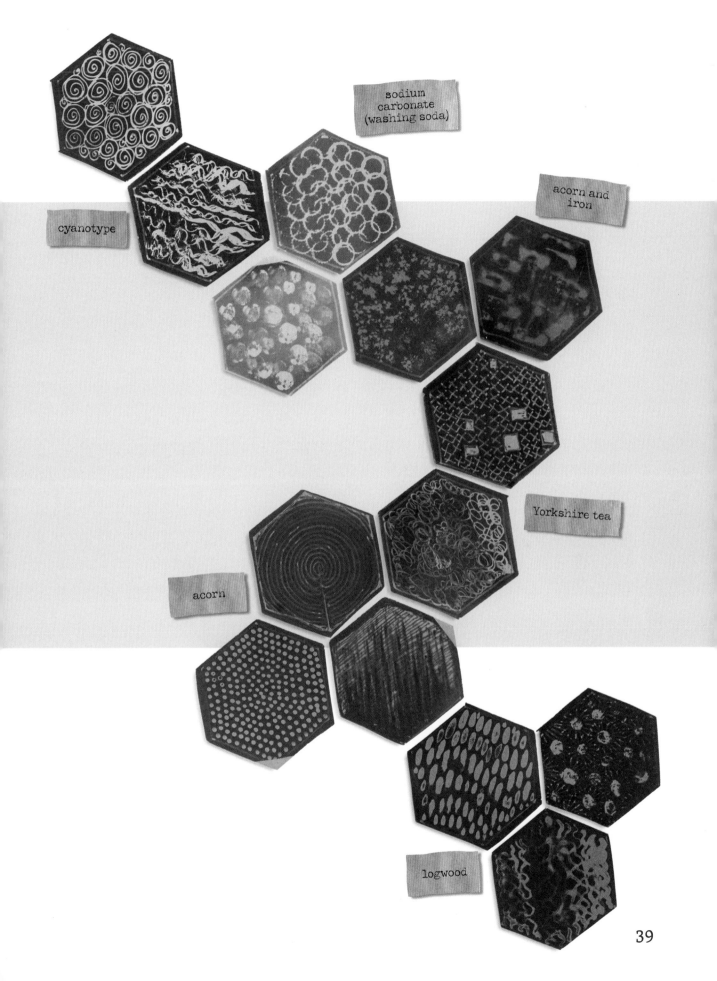

sodium carbonate (washing soda)

acorn and iron

cyanotype

Yorkshire tea

acorn

logwood

Other experiments

☼ **Alter the pH.** It is possible to achieve really different results by changing the pH of the rinsing water. Remember using Litmus paper at school to test things for acidity? A drop of white vinegar or citric acid in the rinse water will acidify the water, which brightens the blues.

☼ **Bleaching cyanotype.** The bleaching effect of sodium carbonate (washing soda) is due to its highly alkaline nature, so it can be used to fade back a print that has come out too dark. It's also great at removing accidental stains on work surfaces, paper and fabrics – see step 2 of the 'Sepia cyanotype' technique on pages 36–39.

FROM LEFT TO RIGHT

Traditional cyanotype, wet cyanotype with sprinkled washing-up liquid (dish soap) bubbles, sepia, traditional cyanotype, traditional cyanotype with gradient exposure, half-traditional cyanotype and half-sepia 'dip-dye', wet cyanotype with washing-up liquid (dish soap) bubbles, sepia, traditional cyanotype.

Adding hydrogen peroxide

You may have seen videos online of people developing cyanotypes that turn very dark blue dramatically when hydrogen peroxide is added in the rinsing stage. This looks great for demonstration purposes and for the YouTube hits, but all that the hydrogen peroxide is doing here is speeding up the development process to intensify the shade of blue. Your prints will gradually darken naturally as they dry and complete the oxidization process.

THE

PROJECTS

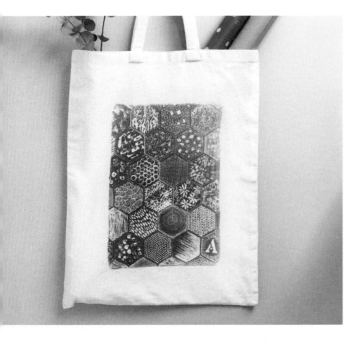

Atkins-style
GREETINGS CARD

Now that you can see how the cyanotype process works, it's time to start discovering why Anna Atkins and Anne Dixon found it so useful in their botanical studies. It's impossible not to be drawn into the magic of printing with natural objects such as leaves and flowers, captured in perfect scale and detail.

Anna Atkins' work was so special because she gave a lot of thought to how the plant specimens were arranged on the paper, to best highlight tiny details. Think about using a small plant with an interesting silhouette, delicate leaf shapes or translucent petals. Common and often overlooked plants, such as daisies, dandelion clocks and grasses, work well; flora with complex silhouettes, such as cow parsley and other umbellifers, look fantastic too.

Consider different ideas for placement on the coated surface: a fern could be arranged to resemble a Christmas tree, for example.

You will need

- Necessities on pages 14–23
- Blank greetings card or thick card/watercolour paper cut and folded to size
- Tracing paper
- Opaque ink fibre-tip pen, stamping ink, letter stamps, stencils and/or dry-transfer letters, for your card message
- Selection of small botanical design elements, such as leaves, small flowers and grasses

Method

1 Prepare your work surface and then make up your solution, as on pages 28 and 29. Coat your card thinly and evenly, especially if you're using card blanks – as these tend to be thin and smooth, they can buckle and curl up easily if they get too wet. Avoid soaking the card and causing bubbles and drips. A sponge brush is good for getting an even coverage. Put the coated card in a dark place and leave to dry.

2 As your coated card is drying, think about the message and composition of your design – if you'd like a little guidance, refer to the photograph opposite. Once you've decided on your arrangement, gather your chosen design elements, including the tracing paper, black fibre-tip pen, stamping ink and/or letter stamps.

3 Cut a small piece of tracing paper (I fed some of mine through a die-cutting machine to make labels, circles and other shapes; tearing the paper would also create an interesting edge) and write, trace or stamp your message using very opaque ink, or with dry-transfer letters.

4 Make your printing 'sandwich': start with a board to support your work; followed by the dry, coated card face up; the tracing paper label face up; your chosen plant(s); and finally a sheet of glass/transparent acrylic (this is an important addition here, as you want the text to be held close to the surface of the card so that it comes out nice and clear).

5 Expose the work for about 20–25 minutes if using a UV lamp, or until the coated surface has turned dusty slate grey in the sun.

6 Rinse and dry the prints, as on page 32. If necessary, press the under some heavy books to flatten them.

TRAVEL JOURNAL

This project is a lovely way to record a day in the garden, a special walk or an occasion, and is something you can keep adding to.

The idea isn't to make 'perfect' prints, but simply to record a moment and take the time to really notice details in a different way. What casts a shadow, and how might that look on paper? It doesn't just have to be natural objects either. You could capture the shadows of a wire fence, a clear plastic food wrapper, a crumpled bottle, bicycle spokes – basically, anything with a strong enough profile to cast a shadow onto your paper.

The simple loose-leaf, ring-binder style journal format makes it easy to add and take out single sheets; it also allows you to include other oddments of print such as fabric scraps and pieces of rejected prints that are too nice to throw away, but make interesting backgrounds for drawing, writing or scrapbooking. The covers are made from mountboard off-cuts, which framers will often let you have cheaply or even for free!

The size of your journal is entirely up to you, based on the dimensions of your journal covers, the size of paper you want to work with, and what you're willing to carry about. If you're going for a long walk you might want to keep things small and portable.

You will need

- Necessities on pages 14–23

- For the journal covers, two mountboard off-cuts or two sheets of smooth white board or two sheets of thick card – mine are 18 x 15cm (7 x 6in). Mountboard is a laminated product, so take care when washing it so that it doesn't get too soggy and fray at the edges. It also tends to be labelled 'archival' and 'acid free', so add a few drops of white vinegar or citric acid to the rinse water in case the pH is too alkaline and affects your print.

- For the journal pages, at least 10 sheets of watercolour paper, about 1cm (⅜in) smaller all around than the journal covers – mine are 17 x 14cm (approx. 6¾ x 5½in)

- Two light-proof bags

- Clipboard and a sheet of transparent acrylic or glass

- Hole punch

- Two 2cm (¾in) diameter loose-leaf ring binder clips

- Piece of round elastic cord, about twice as long as the short side of your book with a little extra to allow you to tie a simple overhand knot

Method

1 Prepare your work surface then make up the solution, as on pages 28 and 29. Coat your journal covers and the journal pages then leave them in a dark place to dry – you could do this the night before your trip. I left spaces on the page deliberately for adding notes later, so play about with how you coat your own pages.

2 When the paper is bone dry and you are ready to go, carefully seal the covers and pages inside one of your light-proof bags, pack your flask of coffee and set off on your adventure!

3 Look for interesting plants and leaves for your design elements. Think about the shadow your chosen plants will cast, the transparency of the leaf or petal, and hold them up to the light and think about the outlines they will make. You don't have to pick the plants but if you do please make sure you have permission and never take more than one. Look for other non-organic, man-made printing opportunities too – remember, anything that casts an interesting shadow could make a print. Once I managed to capture the shadow of an empty glass milk bottle with printed lettering! At the beach, a layer of sand can be swirled and drawn into with your fingers to make intricate patterns.

Continued overleaf > > >

More exposure experiments

After covering your coated paper with your chosen items followed by the transparent acrylic sheet or glass, you can place more plants or objects on top of the sheet of acrylic or glass then remove them halfway through exposure, or at different times. This adds more interest, texture and movement to your piece; you can see how much the paper changes colour too.

4 Before getting your paper out have a rough idea of how you want to arrange your plants/objects. When you're ready, using the clipboard as a base, begin to arrange your design elements on the coated surface of the paper. If it's a still day, experiment with laying plants or objects on the paper without flattening them, to give depth to your print. If it's a windy day, carefully place your flattest items on the coated paper first, lay your sheet of acrylic or glass over all the layers then lay any 3D objects on top. (See also the tip, left.)

5 Leave the work to expose for about 15–20 minutes. The longer you leave a leaf or petal, the more detail will be revealed. In the early stages you'll have only a silhouette, but eventually the light will start to penetrate the leaf or petal, revealing the veins and other details. Interesting-shaped leaves like ferns are perfect for this project, as well as flowers with veined or semi-transparent petals such as geraniums, poppies and buttercups.

6 After exposing your print, quickly pop the pages/cover into the second light-proof bag to stop further oxidization.

7 Repeat steps 3–6 until you've printed all your pages and covers.

8 When you return home, rinse and dry the prints, as on page 32. If necessary, press your prints under something heavy after drying to flatten them, such as a large book.

9 When everything is dry and pressed, begin to assemble your journal by punching two holes in each page and the two cover boards evenly. Clip everything together using the metal rings. Punch a small hole in the middle of the back cover, along the short edge opposite the rings. Thread both ends of the elastic through the hole, from the printed side to the unprinted side, then tie the ends into a knot. This elastic will hold the book closed.

10 To finish, add further text, other small cyanotype experiments or little envelopes to store found objects, seeds and other mementoes from your day.

CONCERTINA JOURNAL

Play around with the format of your nature journal, as it doesn't have to be in a notebook. Here, I stitched together my pages along the longest edges only, to create a concertina-style display of my finds. I then added some free-machine stitching and hand embroidery to some of the pages, to add extra textures and embellishments.

Topiary Garden
POP-UP CARD

This project builds on the basic idea you've already seen in action
in the previous projects, that different shades of blue can be achieved
through longer or shorter exposure times.

By using paper shapes that form a kind of 'jigsaw' on top of coated
paper then removing them one by one at intervals, you can build up
multi-hued images.

The creative possibilities with this method are limited only by your
paper-cutting skills!

You will need

- Necessities on pages 14–23

- Thick paper or blank greetings card – I used Khadi paper cards and envelopes

- Card for stencils – this could be cut from upcycled packaging such as an old cereal box

- Tracing paper and pencil, and scanned (or traced) copy of the template on page 107

- Scissors, a craft knife and a cutting mat

- Tweezers or a pin, for removing very small foreground templates

- Optional: design elements, such as grasses or pressed flowers

- Optional: embroidery thread in your chosen colour, and an embroidery/crewel needle

Method

1 Open out your card flat in front of you, so that the folded crease is in the middle, horizontally (see the blue dotted lines in the right-hand diagram).

2 Print or trace the template onto the stencil card and cut around and above the blue dotted and black dashed lines.

3 Line up the stencil template so that the house is sitting on the fold of your card then lightly draw around it. Using a craft knife, cut around the house and the top of the hills only (see the black dashed outline, in the right-hand diagram). Note that you don't cut right to the edges of the card (you'll cut the card in half!); start where the blue dotted line touches the hills. When you have finished cutting and the card is folded and standing up, the house and hills will 'pop' up.

4 Refold the card. Prepare your work surface then make up your solution, as on pages 28 and 29. Coat the front of the card with the cyanotype solution then leave it to dry while you cut out the rest of the template shapes for the landscape in front of the house, using the stencil. Remember to number each piece, referring to the diagram on the right, so that you know how to piece your jigsaw puzzle of garden shapes.

5 Once your card is dry, lay it flat on a board, making sure you are working away from bright light. Place your jigsaw pieces over the coated paper, as shown. You won't need a sheet of transparent acrylic or glass here, as you'll be moving things around. It's a bit fiddly but don't be too worried about slightly misaligned jigsaw pieces; it all adds to the individual nature of the design.

Continued overleaf > > >

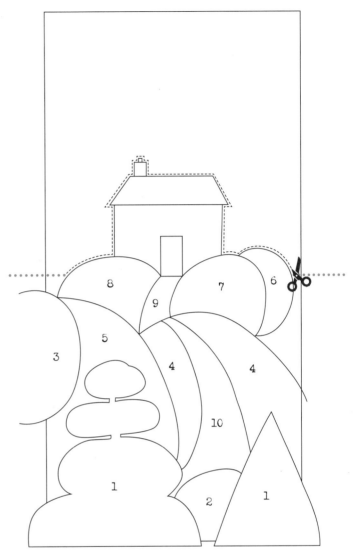

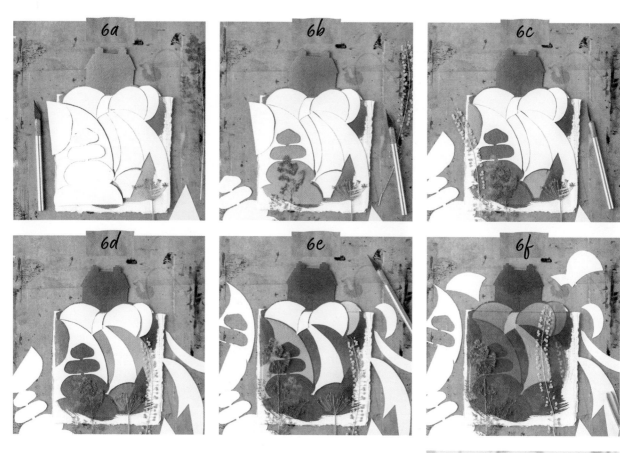

6 Place your work under a UV lamp (see the tip, right, if you want to work outside). Using your tweezers, a pin, the tip of a craft knife or a steady hand, and going from 1 to 10, remove the numbered pieces one by one over the course of the exposure time (roughly 20–25 minutes in total), allowing around 2–3 minutes between each moved piece. I don't tend to time each stage exactly; I just watch the coated paper change colour, and once there's an obvious change I move another piece. The path pieces stay on the longest. As I removed the immediate foreground pieces, I replaced them with grasses or pressed flowers to add texture and interest.

7 Rinse and dry your card as on page 32. If necessary, place the card under something heavy to flatten it.

8 To finish, you can cut out the door section completely, or cut one side edge and the top and bottom edges so it can swing open and give the impression of light flowing from an open doorway, lighting up the path. For one of my cards, I decided to add embroidered details in rust-coloured embroidery thread – French knots and cross-stitches for the heart motif, running stitch for the 'trail' marks along the path, and a single cross-stitch 'kiss' in the bottom-right corner.

Working outside

If it's a still day, and you aren't going to get frustrated with the wind moving things before you're ready, you can work outside. Be aware that you will need to work more quickly outside too.

60

Trompe L'oeil
LACE PURSE

Printing on fabric uses the same basic techniques as using paper but with a few small differences – see pages 20–22 for a reminder on how to print on fabric.

I find the results of cyanotype printing on fabric are often even more beautiful and striking than on paper, and it's great for embellishing with embroidery or, in this case, mimicking hand-made lace.

For this project I've used a ready-made purse blank made from 100% organic cotton (see the suppliers list on page 108 for recommendations).

You will need

- ☼ Necessities on pages 14–23. As fabric absorbs the solution much more than paper does, you may need to make up a larger volume of solution
- ☼ Purse blank made from 100% cotton
- ☼ Vintage lace or paper doily
- ☼ Newsprint or card, to put inside the purse while you coat it
- ☼ Optional: embellishments for your purse, from zip pulls and embroidery designs to labels. I've added a silk zip pull to my purse, as well as a personal label.

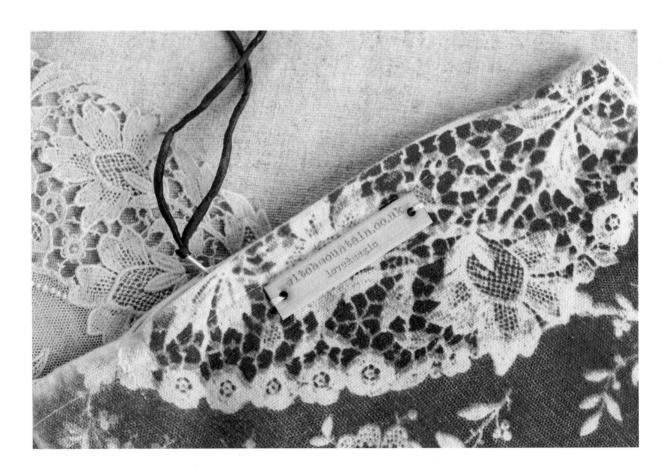

Method

1 Wash, dry then iron the purse. Washing removes any finishes on the fabric, added during the manufacturing stage.

2 Fold a piece of newsprint or card then pop it inside the purse blank to stop the solution staining the back and inside. Make sure to remove this before the rinsing stage! Prepare your work surface then make up your solution, as on pages 28 and 29. Then, carefully use a foam or hake brush to coat one side of your purse.

Note that coating fabric is not always as smooth and easy as coating paper, and uses more solution. You might find you need to load your brush more but, at the same time, you need to avoid splashing and over-soaking the fabric because you want it to dry fast and evenly. Remember the solution will continue to spread as it works through the fibres so, depending on your fabric choice, it's not always easy to get a straight outline or perfect shape.

3 Lay the coated purse flat on a protected surface then leave it in a dark place to dry. You could peg up the corners and hang the purse for drying, but make sure it hangs somewhere dark and the surface below is protected from any drips. You need your coated purse to be completely dry, before proceeding to the next stage – see the tip box, right.

4 Once the purse is dry, arrange the lace on top of the coated fabric. Cover the lace and purse with a sheet of transparent acrylic or glass for good contact, and for a crisper print. Expose for at least 25 minutes if you are using a UV lamp. If you rinse too soon, you risk getting a pale and washed-out result, like faded 1970s denim (which isn't always a bad thing).

5 Rinse the purse, as on page 32. Washing the solution out is easier than with paper because you can squeeze the fabric and make sure you've completely rinsed away the chemicals; you can also use warm water after the initial wash in cold water.

6 Hang to dry. Remember that the blue will continue to darken as it dries. Iron the purse before adding any other embellishments like zip pulls, labels, and so on.

Optional

Once dry, you can repeat the process on the other side of the purse, if you wish.

Drying your fabric

It's important to allow your fabric to dry after coating it with your solution. This is so you can achieve a crisp print that doesn't wash out at the rinsing stage, but also to avoid getting the solution on your piece of beautiful lace.

The drying process for fabric can take a while, and this is the part that I find the hardest because my studio isn't very warm. The longer it takes, the more you risk light and oxygen starting to oxidize the solution. Working at night under normal light bulbs, then leaving the fabric to dry overnight in a dark drawer (lined with paper) should be fine. If you are willing to invest in one, the ideal would be a proper print-drying rack in a warm, dark room.

If you discover that your coated fabric has started to darken as it dries, don't panic – try printing with it anyway. I've had some nice results from unpromising-looking beginnings!

'Picnic in the Woods' CUTLERY ROLL

This design is based on a pencil case my mum made for me when I was at primary/elementary school. It's also very simple to sew because I'm not great with a sewing machine... or anything that involves measuring and straight lines, really! Besides, luckily this book is about printing not sewing.

The focus of this project is playing with and using more three-dimensional objects for printing. As this is a cutlery roll, I loved the idea of using the actual cutlery for the printing pattern! A variation might be to make a crafter's tool roll or artist's pencil case; so, if picnics aren't your thing, have a look-about for some interesting objects on your chosen theme – scissors, paint or make-up brushes, crochet hooks and so on.

Experiment with moving around your chosen items during exposure, which will add depth to your design and combine all the techniques we've used so far.

You will need

- Necessities on pages 14–23. As fabric absorbs the solution much more than paper does, you may need to make up a larger volume of solution

- 100% pure cotton fabric – I've used printer's mediumweight cotton for the final piece; if you'd like to experiment with the design before committing to a more expensive fabric, I recommend using unbleached calico for your test samples as this is relatively cheap

- Mix of man-made and natural design elements, including interesting cutlery (look out for serrated knives and fancy teaspoons), grasses and/or pressed flowers

- Optional: lace or paper doily

- Sewing machine and thread

- Fabric scissors

- Ribbon or fabric tape

- Optional: embroidery/crewel needle and embroidery threads in your chosen colours

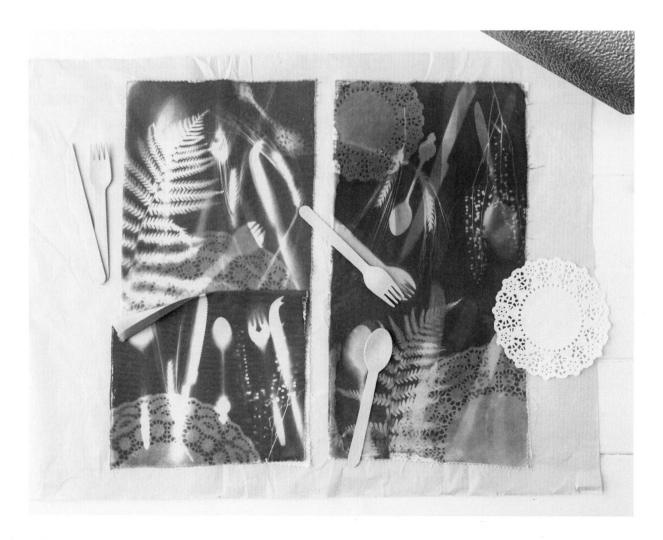

Method

1 After washing and ironing your fanric, cut three shapes from it – two measuring 25 x 22cm (17¾ x 8¾in) and one 20 x 22cm (8 x 8¾in). One large piece will be the inside of the cutlery roll, the other large piece the outside of the cutlery roll. The smallest piece is for the pocket.

2 Prepare your work surface then make up your solution, as on pages 28 and 29. Carefully coat one side of all three pieces. Note that the bottom half of the large inside piece will be covered by the smallest pocket piece, so you don't have to coat that one all the way down. Leave to dry completely in a dark place.

3 Gather then arrange your design elements over the coated fabric. Because you're using three-dimensional objects, you won't be able to lay a sheet of transparent acrylic or glass over your design, so work in a space where the wind won't blow things around. Place the flattest objects on the fabric first – I've used some grasses and ferns to soften the design; for another sample, shown opposite, I used a paper doily too. Then place your cutlery, and/or any other three-dimensional objects, on top.

Expose the fabric for at least 25 minutes if indoors under a UV lamp, or until it has turned a dusty blue-grey colour outside. Be aware of the angle of your light source and the shadows cast by your objects, especially if you're working outside: three-dimensional objects will make prints with ghostly shadows, like an offset lino print, depending on where and how they're placed. You can add to this effect by slightly moving items halfway through the exposure – you could move all the cutlery and leave the plants for the last 5 minutes, or vice versa.

4 Rinse the fabric, as on page 32. Soak and rinse the fabric again until the water runs clear and hang to dry before ironing.

5 This is an optional stage: before using the sewing machine to stitch everything together, I added some simple hand embroidery in a contrasting colour. I drew faint pencil outlines on my fabric, to give me a guide when outlining shapes with running stitch. I also added some French knots here and there. Add as little or as much detail as you like (to see the embroidery on the finished design, see page 70).

6 Fold over the top edge of the pocket piece twice by 5mm (¼in), press and sew two lines of top-stitching along the fold, on the right side of the fabric, to create a neat hem. (Also see the fold at the top of the pocket piece in the photograph opposite.)

Continued overleaf > > >

7 Place the hemmed pocket on top of the large inside piece (and over the uncoated area, if you left this unpainted), with both printed sides facing up and the raw, unhemmed edge of the pocket lined up with the bottom edge of the large inside piece. Pin the layers together then, using your sewing machine and coordinating thread, stitch four to five evenly spaced vertical lines over the pocket, through the large inside piece at the same time. These lines will make little compartments in your pocket for your cutlery or other items. Make sure to stitch just over the bottom line of top-stitching, and to reverse/back-stitch at this end of your stitch lines to make the tops of the compartments extra secure.

8 Pin your tape or ribbon to the right-hand side of your stitched pieces, about a quarter of the way up and facing inwards. Place your large outside piece over the ribbon or tape and stitched layers, the printed side facing down. Both right sides should now be 'hidden' inside, with the tape or ribbon sandwiched in between. Make sure the tape or ribbon is tucked inside away from the edges, with a hint of a short tail showing on the outside.

9 Stitch all around the cutlery roll with a 5mm (¼in) seam allowance, leaving an approximate 5cm (2in) gap at one end for turning the roll right side out. Trim across the corners at an angle, to reduce bulk, then turn everything the right way out. Press the allowance of the opening to the inside by 5mm (¼in) then stitch the gap closed by top-stitching all around the perimeter of the cutlery roll. Now plan what to put in your picnic hamper...

Back of the closed cutlery roll.

Front of the closed cutlery roll.

'Patchwork'
TOTE BAG

Mark-making is a classic art school exercise! I really enjoyed spending an hour or so doodling, smudging and playing with different materials and tools to see what kind of effect they produced when printed.

Absolutely no drawing skill is needed here because the aim is to create a grid of different textures, patterns and marks using various opaque media, giving you an idea of how you can use hand-drawn techniques to print with in future.

The designs could also be printed on paper, but for this project I felt they worked nicely as a print on fabric – the marks combined with the fabric remind me of a cross between a patchwork blanket and a traditional embroidery sampler.

You will need

- Necessities on pages 14–23. Note you may need more solution than usual, as fabric soaks up a lot of solution

- 100% pure cotton tote bag

- Large sheet of paper or card, to put inside the bag to stop the solution seeping through

- Selection of media to design and/or 'draw' with, which will work on the shiny surface of the acetate without rubbing off – markers, pens, stamps, inkpads, paints, oil pastels, etc.

- Sheets of acetate on which to apply your chosen media

- Optional: traced hexagon template on page 106, patchwork template or a ruler and pen, for marking out a grid

- Optional: Gutta outliner, to make a border

- Optional: test paper, to check your markings before committing to fabric

- Optional: embroidery/crewel needle and embroidery threads in your chosen colours

 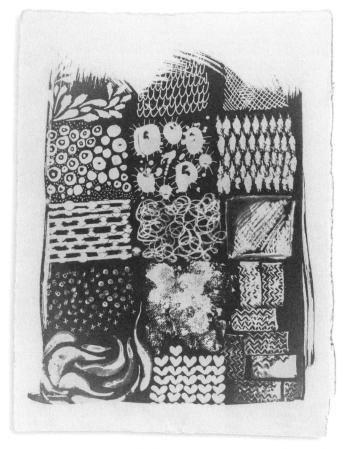

Test marks for a sample, from acetate (left) to print (right). Note that the way the solution is applied can add a painterly effect to your cyanotype background.

Method

1 Wash, dry then iron the bag, to remove any finishes.

2 Prepare your work surface then make up your solution, as on pages 28 and 29. Coat a large area on the centre front of your bag with the cyanotype solution, remembering to put some paper inside the bag to stop the solution seeping through to the back. Use the size of your acetate as a guide for how large an area you need to paint with the solution: you need to ensure that your coated area is a little smaller than the acetate, so that the edges of the sheet don't leave an outline when exposed and the whole coated area is covered by your design. Straight edges can be difficult to achieve on fabric but you could try using silk painting Gutta outliner to contain the solution if you want a certain shape. Once coated, place the bag in a dark place and leave the fabric to dry completely.

3 Gather your chosen media to create your marks. Permanent markers such as Staedtler Lumocolor Marker Pens; Indian ink; window markers, such as Posca Pens; acrylic paint; soft oil pastels and wax crayons (Kitpas Window Crayons work nicely, and these can also be used with water to make a 'paint' for watercolour effects); and solvent-based ink pads. The colour isn't important: we're interested only in the variations of opacity and the shadows cast by the marks that these different types of media make. Also think about the tools you're going to use to make your marks – brushes, pens, stencils and stamps – as these will create different textures and effects in tandem with your media.

4 Either trace the hexagon template in the back of the book, use a ruler to draw a simple grid of squares on your acetate, or draw little boxes or 'compartments' freehand. If you want to get fancy you could use an actual patchwork template to make a framework for your mark-making.

Continued overleaf > > >

5 Now here's the fun part! Put aside your worries about perfection and whether or not you can draw, take a deep breath and fill each compartment with a different pattern, mark or stamp. Try not to overthink it. I've used: pen lids dipped in Indian ink, lino blocks dipped in Posca ink, inky fingerprints, ink splats, wax crayon scribbles, Indian ink with water pens, letter stamps and stencils, 'scrim' fabric with ink, dots, cross-hatching and stripes. The possibilities for drawing and creating painterly negatives can be seen clearly as you do this: as you don't have to reverse text or images for cyanotype printing, the process makes it very easy to transfer designs from sketchbooks or templates.

6 If you want to make a test print on paper first, go ahead and do that now. If you like the effect, print your tote bag, exposing for around 25 minutes under a UV lamp or according to light levels if you're printing outside.

7 Rinse the fabric, as on page 32. Continue soaking and rinsing until the water runs clear and hang to dry before ironing.

Optional

I stitched details onto the design on page 73, using chain stitch to outline a few of the hexagon edges.

OPPOSITE
This bag was made using printed circles from a pen lid dipped in ink, a letter stencil and stamps, Indian ink, fine marker pens, and doodles made with Posca pens.

Fabric
NIGHT LIGHTS

This is the question I get asked the most: 'OK, I get how you've printed with plants, but how did you get the hare/fox/bear on there?' As you'll have seen in the previous project, making a hand-drawn acetate negative is the simplest way of transforming your own artwork into a cyanotype print. You can create a negative directly on the acetate, or you can easily trace something from your sketchbook or a copyright-free image.

By now you may be aware that whatever is opaque will print white: 'if it blocks light, it will be white; if it lets the light through, it will be blue'. This means hand-drawn negative lines will come out white. If you have images or shapes with more complex and/or subtle outlines, it will be difficult to transfer your design onto acetate. The answer is to make a digital negative.

By scanning and editing your drawings on a computer then printing onto a special film for inkjet or laser printers, you can use elements from your sketchbooks and photographs then edit them to create digital negatives. I use Adobe® Photoshop® to edit my images, but there are lots of other free photo-editing apps such as GIMP and even Microsoft Paint!

You will need to convert your image to black and white then invert it before printing it onto the special acetate. You may want to print the whole image, but with a photo-editing app you can also select only part of your drawing or photograph to create a motif that can be used in lots of different compositions.

These little night lights are a nice way of creating and displaying personally designed prints for your home or for the special people in your life.

You will need

- Necessities on pages 14–23. Note you may need more solution than usual, as fabric soaks up a lot of solution

- Approximately 50cm (19¾in) by width of fabric of natural fabric (I used poplin cotton here), depending on the size of your lampshade panel

- A lampshade-making kit – I use Dannells® as one kit has enough supplies for several lampshades

- A3 (297 x 420mm/11¾ x 16½in) or A4 (210 x 297mm/US Letter/8¼ x 11¾in) sheet of clear inkjet- or laser-friendly contact-negative film on which to print your artwork

- Your artwork, drawn digitally or scanned from a sketchbook

- Grasses and flowers, for additional design elements

- Optional: hare motif on page 106, to print onto the laser- and inkjet-friendly film

- Fabric scissors

- Optional: pinking shears

- Double-sided tape

- Optional: bradawl or hole punch, for embroidery-stitch holes

- Optional: embroidery/crewel needle and stranded embroidery threads in your chosen colours

- LED tealights – do not use real tealights!

Tech-free night light

If you don't have access to any digital tools such as a printer, you could still make the lantern by tracing the template onto tracing paper or onto clear acetate with an opaque marker.

Method

1 Wash, dry then iron your fabric, to remove any finishes. Centre the clear sticky-backed sheet from the lampshade kit on top – don't remove the protective film on the backing yet; you are simply using it as a template. Cut your fabric, leaving 2–3cm (¾–1in) extra around the edges to allow for shrinkage and trimming.

2 Prepare your work surface then make up your solution, as on pages 28 and 29. Coat the fabric thinly and evenly. You may not need to coat the whole fabric, depending on your design. Leave it to dry completely in a dark place.

3 Scan your artwork (or my design on page 106) and open it within your photo-editing app. Convert to black and white then invert it to make a negative, adjusting the lighting if necessary. Print it onto the clear inkjet- or laser-friendly contact-negative film. Make sure to use the recommended settings supplied by the brand and that the design is landscape in format. There is no need to print in mirror image or reverse any writing.

Unless you have access to an A3 (297 x 420mm/ 11¾ x 16½in) printer, you will probably need to print your chosen design on an A4 (210 x 297mm/US Letter/ 8¼ x 11¾in) size sheet, which you will find is (annoyingly) slightly smaller than your lantern fabric.

This is important to bear in mind, as the edges of the film will leave lines in the final print; however, these can be easily disguised and covered up with leaves and plants in the next step (see the fern leaves in the photograph below).

4 When you're ready to print, lay out your work on a flat surface and arrange your design elements on top of the coated surface, using transparent acrylic or glass to hold them in place for sharper images. For my print, I placed some natural design elements on top of the sheet of acrylic or glass that I planned to remove halfway through exposure to add depth and a feeling of movement; these result in less defined prints, but are good if you like subtle foreground interest.

5 Expose the fabric for around 20–25 minutes with a UV lamp, or slightly less if you're working outside on a bright, sunny day. By now you will have an idea about what to look for and can gauge when a print is 'cooked', but my best results seem to be when I leave it for longer than I think it needs!

Continued overleaf > > >

6 Rinse the fabric, as on page 32. Soak and rinse the fabric again until the water runs clear and hang to dry before ironing.

7 You can then follow the assembly instructions that come with the kit. Place your lovely fabric face down on the table then lay the lampshade backing on top once again, positioning it so that the hare sits in the right place (along the edge where the bottom of the backing can be peeled away). When you're happy with the positioning, remove the protective film from the backing and stick it in place (making sure it's stuck to the wrong side of the fabric, or you'll be very cross!). Smooth out any bubbles or creases. Using the backing as a guide, trim away the excess fabric using very sharp scissors on the short edges and, ideally, pinking shears on the long edges to avoid fraying. Note that, on one short end, I have left an allowance of 5mm (¼in) to fold over in the next step.

8 Peel off the long strips of excess backing on the long edges to reveal the top and bottom edges of the fabric, which will eventually be folded over to make the rolled edges. Fold the short fabric edge with the allowance over the backing and stick it in place with double-sided tape (which is provided in the kit). Then stick another length of double-sided tape on top of the folded fabric; this will make a neat seam when the fabric is rolled up.

9 Wrap the lampshade rings with double-sided tape then line these up with the top and bottom edges of the backing. Starting from the short end without the folded-over edge, roll the rings to the other short end, rolling up the fabric at the same time. You should end up with the neat seam on top, and the double-sided tape securing the roll in place.

10 Once rolled and secure, fold over the fabric allowance on the long edges then use the tool supplied with the kit to push the long edges under the rings, to neaten.

Optional

I like to add stitching to the closed edge of the night light, for decoration and to make sure it stays rolled up.

Carefully make 12 holes in the assembled lantern with the help of a bradawl – six holes down one side of the long 'seam', and six down the other. Using your chosen embroidery thread and an embroidery/crewel needle, stitch cross-stitches through the holes, as shown above, to finish off your night light.

Alternative ideas

When I'm not using it as an electric candle lantern, sometimes I use my night light as a cover for a 'jam jar bouquet', to hold small plant pots of kitchen herbs, or as a desk tidy.

Portraits and
PICTURES

If your interest in cyanotype leans more towards photographic uses, and things like D-max (maximum density in a print) really matters to you, then there is a wonderful world of technical detail for you to discover through cyanotype printing. In this project, I will give you the basics you need to print photographs using cyanotype.

As you have seen in the previous project, you can make and print negatives of artwork using the cyanotype process by laying an inverted image over your coated background. The same can be done with a photograph: invert the image in your photo-editing app, then print this on special contact-negative film using a normal inkjet or laser printer. This method works particularly well with simple high-contrast images that would also look good printed in black and white.

Most of us are used to messing about with photography filters on apps, so you may already know that some things look great in monochrome and others just don't. This means you'll need to consider your choice of image carefully. If you're taking a photograph specially for cyanotype printing, think about the lighting and the background. These days, it's also really easy to delete or select particular objects in a photograph and remove background clutter.

For this project I chose a favourite picture of my daughter, and used a photo-editing app to adjust the lighting and remove the background. I thought it would be nice to make my portrait sepia too, like a vintage photograph from a family album.

You will need

- Necessities on pages 14–23. Note you may need more solution than usual, as fabric soaks up a lot of solution

- Square of natural fabric – I used mediumweight cotton measuring approx. 25cm (10in) square

- Inkjet printer and clear inkjet-friendly film (such as Digital Contact Film or OHP film)

- JPEG of your chosen photograph, with good tonal range

- Additional design elements that complement your photo – these could be leaves and flowers, or maybe objects connected to the subject of your photo

- Sodium carbonate (washing soda) and teabags (or another source of tannic acid) for sepia toning

- Optional: embroidery/crewel needle and stranded embroidery threads in your chosen colours

- Optional: wooden embroidery hoop or poster hanger, for display – if you decide to use an embroidery hoop, note you can also stain the wood of the hoop using cyanotype solution, for a coordinating result

Method

1 Edit your photo in your chosen app; I'm using Adobe® Photoshop®. You need to end up with a photo that's black and white and inverted, as seen opposite. (For more information on editing photos, please see the tip, right.)

2 Print your photo, using the settings that come with your chosen film. Remember all you have learnt so far: the black areas will be white when printed, and the clear areas will print blue. Use a high-quality print setting, if possible, so that the negative doesn't come out streaky. As mentioned in the previous project, there is no need to print mirror image or reverse any writing. However, do check the size of the document before pressing 'print' – you want to make sure it's the right size for your hoop or poster frame! Once your photo-negative is printed, wait a short while before using it to make sure the ink is dry.

3 Wash, dry then iron your fabric. Prepare your work surface then make up your solution, as on pages 28 and 29. Coat your square of fabric evenly with a thin layer of solution then leave it to dry completely in a dark place.

4 Arrange your photo-negative and any extra design elements over your coated fabric. When using negatives, I recommend always laying a sheet of transparent acrylic or glass over the top to ensure there is close contact between the film and your coated surface.

5 Expose the fabric for around 20–25 minutes with a UV lamp, or less if you're working outside on a bright, sunny day.

6 Rinse the fabric, as on page 32. Soak and rinse the fabric again until the water runs clear and hang to dry before ironing.

Continued overleaf > > >

Editing your photos

Whichever app you use to edit your photo, the instructions will basically be the same – it's just that the tools will be in slightly different places, and the names may be slightly different to the ones below. I'm not a photographer but I love messing about with images, so just trust your own judgement and enjoy experimenting.

– If you want to **remove the background**, make sure the layer it is on is selected, click 'object selection tool' then either copy and paste the selection onto a new blank document, or click on 'Select' > 'Inverse' > 'Delete'.

– If you want to **change the shape of your image so it's circular** (to fit into a hoop), click 'Elliptical Marquee Tool' > 'Select' > 'Inverse' > 'Delete'. You may be presented with an option to fill in the background; simply select 'White' under 'Contents' then click 'OK'.

– Now **convert the image into black and white**, if it's not already. Click 'Image' > 'Adjustments' > 'Black & White' (or 'Desaturate'). Select 'Maximum Black' from the drop-down menu, if you have that choice. At this point you can play about with the levels and adjust the contrast if you feel confident, to make sure you have a nice tonal range.

– Finally, **invert the image**, if it's not already. Click 'Image' > 'Adjustments' > 'Invert'.

7 I chose to turn my blueprint sepia. Once your print is developed and dry, prepare your tannin dye bath in one bowl (this could be simply very strong black or green tea that has been allowed to cool) then in another bowl mix a weak solution of sodium carbonate (washing soda) and lukewarm water – see page 36 for notes on quantities and volumes. This will create a very alkaline solution that will bleach out the Prussian blue, turning it pale violet to golden yellow.

Soak your print in the sodium carbonate solution, pulling it out every few seconds or so to check the change in colour. When the print has noticeably faded, rinse the print in clear water before placing it in your prepared tannin dye bath. Leave it in there until it reaches the desired sepia tone.

Optional

As a final touch, I added embellishments to my portrait with some hand-stitching (see the close-up photograph above). Using cream embroidery thread, I 'scattered' seed stitches throughout the whole background area behind my main subjects.

Warning

Make sure you keep the equipment you've used to mix the washing soda well away from the rest of your cyanotype things – paper, developing trays and so on – to avoid contaminating them with the strong alkaline solution, which could lead to spoilt future prints.

OPPOSITE

The framed image shows a sepia print, on fabric, of a woodland photograph with a quote by the naturalist and conservationist, John Muir. The hoop is a tiny version of the portrait of my daughter, with contrasting hand-stitching as a final embellishment.

'Hag Stone'
JEWELLERY

Earlier, I explained how cyanotype can be applied not only to paper and fabric, but other surfaces too – see page 23 for a reminder.

There are so many unique and creative ways that artists and photographers have used cyanotype to experiment with printing on many different surfaces. I've kept this project fairly simple by using an unsual surface that I know your cyanotype solution will 'stick' to. If you enjoy printing on clay, don't be afraid to explore other surfaces – you never know what you might discover.

'Hag stones' or 'witch stones' are the inspiration for these brooches and pendants. Traditionally, a hag stone is a small stone or pebble with a naturally occurring water-worn hole. They are used as a good luck charm to ward off evil spirits, worries or bad dreams, as they are too big to fit through the hole!

You will need

- Necessities on pages 14–23. You won't need much solution, as a little goes a long way with this technique
- Air-dry (modelling) clay – I use the one by DAS®
- Baking/parchment paper, on which to work your clay
- Optional: rolling pin and chosen cookie cutters – for the holes in the middle, you can use a small round object such as a pen lid or old thimble for larger holes, or the sharp end of an old needle for a smaller hole
- Chosen design elements – I've used flowers and grasses, but textures like lace or wrapped threads would work well too

- Kitchen paper
- Brooch backs, jewellery cords, contrasting embroidery thread and other findings
- Cold wax medium (such as the one by Gamblin, or another suitable varnish) – I have previously used a craft polyurethane gloss, which works well, but always test a small area whenever using a new material for the first time
- Tissue paper, for polishing

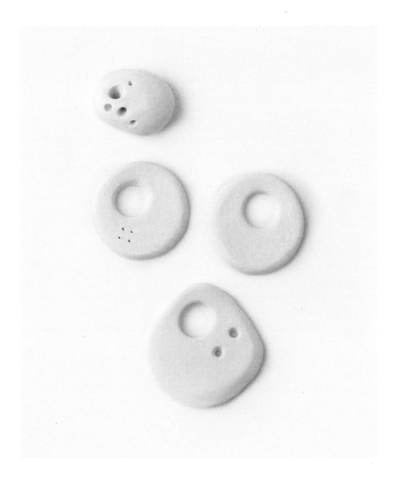

Method

1 First you need to make your clay shapes. Create these on baking/ parchment paper, as this will stop the clay sticking to your work surface. You can either make irregular flat pebble shapes by hand; or, you can use a rolling pin to roll out pieces of clay that are about 0.5–1cm (¼–⅜in) thick, then use a cookie cutter to cut out your chosen shapes.

2 Make holes of various sizes in the shapes, for hanging and for decoration. If you want to stitch into your piece later, note that it's also fairly easy to push a needle through when the shapes are just dry but not fully set – see step 8 on page 96.

3 Leave the clay shapes uncovered on a flat surface until they're completely dry – this can take a day or two.

4 Once dry, prepare your work surface then make up your solution, as on pages 28 and 29. I used my usual recipe, but many people recommend a 50:50 mix of Ferric Ammonium Citrate and Potassium Ferricyanide for air-dry clay, so try that too. Use a sponge brush to very lightly coat one side of your clay shape with cyanotype solution. The idea is to coat the surface, but not allow too much solution to soak into the clay: if you have to rinse the clay for too long, there's a risk your lovely shape will get too soggy and fragile.

5 Let the surface dry for a few minutes and then arrange your design – in these examples I've used tiny pieces of foliage but you could use lace, die-cut confetti shapes or negatives from previous projects. The surface of my clay was smooth and flat so I could still balance a sheet of glass on top to keep things pressed down, but if your shapes are rounder you could use cling film/plastic food wrap to hold your objects in close contact with the clay.

6 Expose the shapes for at least 30 minutes under a UV lamp or slightly longer than normal in bright sunlight. I've found that the best results are achieved with a much longer exposure.

Continued overleaf > > >

7 Rinsing is a delicate process: because the clay's surface will soften in the water, the print is vulnerable to damage while it's wet. To prevent the latter from happening, try to handle your shapes by their edges.

Place the printed shapes in a tray of cold water, leave them to soak for a little bit, gently swish them then take them out of the water. Repeat the process, changing the water each time, until the water stays clear and has no trace of yellow in it. Carefully lay your work on a piece of kitchen roll, dabbing the surface to carefully soak up excess water. I found that yellow solution continued to leach out of the clay for ages (out of proportion to the amount I'd used!), so check your shapes after a few minutes and rinse again if you need to. The kitchen paper really seemed to help draw the remaining liquid out of the clay.

8 When your clay shape is almost fully dry, you can add holes for stitched details. Then, when it's totally dry, seal it with a coat of varnish. I used Gamblin cold wax medium, which has a very tactile application – you can rub it on with your fingers, and then it can be polished to a velvety, semi-matt sheen using tissue paper.

9 Finally, you can add your embellishments and fastenings. Use contrasting thread to wrap, embroider or weave on your thread details. If you are making a brooch, glue on the brooch back using a multi-purpose adhesive. For a necklace, thread a ribbon or cord through the holes or the wrapped thread. Or, leave your shapes as they are and keep them as talismans, under your pillow, to keep away nightmares.

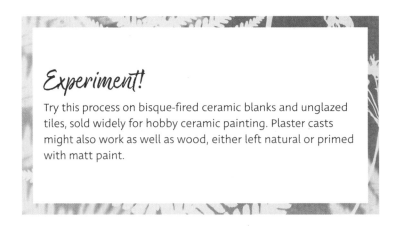

Experiment!

Try this process on bisque-fired ceramic blanks and unglazed tiles, sold widely for hobby ceramic painting. Plaster casts might also work as well as wood, either left natural or primed with matt paint.

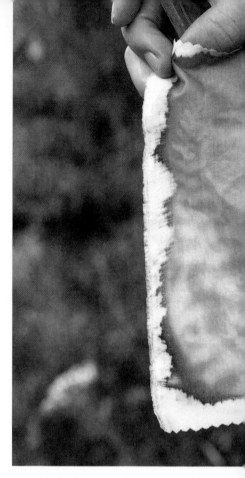

RIGHT
This piece demonstrates a print on fabric that wasn't
exposed for long enough (or where the light source
wasn't strong enough), and so the image was partially
washed out during the rinsing stage.

'Toil and trouble...':
WHEN THINGS
GO 'WRONG'

In my own work, and in taking on the task of writing this book, the thing I keep having to remind myself is that all creativity is about experimenting and discovering, about learning from 'mistakes' and adjusting expectations according to actual results.

It can be frustrating if you have a definite, fixed idea of how you want things to look but they don't turn out as intended. It's not always obvious why, either, when you're working with a sensitive chemical process that has many variables. However, sometimes the unexpected 'mistakes' can turn out better than the technically perfect prints because they have a certain 'mystery' about them – in the same way that a rough sketch can often have more life about it than a finished painting.

It's important to remember that the cyanotype solution can react easily to contaminants and changes in pH balance. Tiny changes in light levels, timings and rinsing water can also affect the results. This can make it very hard to give definitive instructions, let alone make an edition of identical prints. However, it's this unpredicatability that makes the process so absorbing and versatile – as appealing to a meticulous photographer as it is to an artist who is more interested in experimental mark-making, or creating a surface for stitch or multi-media artwork.

What happened?	Why?	Try this...
Print washes away or appears very pale.	Underexposed.	Leave in the light for longer and look out for the dusty grey/blue colour. It's always best to err towards leaving things longer than you think you need to.
Print washes away or appears very pale.	Paper or fabric not fully dry before exposure.	Make sure the printing surface is completely dry before exposure.
Print washes away or appears very pale.	Too alkaline (either the printing surface or the rinsing water).	– Add a few drops of white vinegar or citric acid to the rinsing water. – It could be that the paper/fabric is just not suitable. The paper/fabric could be pre-soaked in acidified water but this is a lot of effort when there are so many alternatives. – Try adding 3% hydrogen peroxide to the final rinse bath. Prints will continue to darken over 24 hours as they dry but adding hydrogen peroxide will speed this up.
Light areas continue to darken or stains appear on the back.	Some solution remains in the paper.	Make sure to soak and rinse your printed surface well to allow all the solution to wash out.
Purple or violet stains.	Especially on fabrics, this can be because it wasn't fully dry before printing or because of mystery contaminants in the fabric. This can also happen when printing on damp paper with fresh foliage in warm sunlight, as humidity builds up under the glass.	– Embrace the unpredictable purple! – Ensure the fabric is clean before coating, and dries quickly and evenly. – Apply your design elements as soon as possible after coating your surface. – Work in a clean space to avoid contamination with alkaline substances. – A wash in warm/hot water can sometimes remove the purple, or you may find it disappears once fully dry.

What happened?	Why?	Try this...
Spots and patches.	Uneven coating, air bubbles in the rinse process or random contamination.	Be sure to swish the print about in the rinse water to make sure there are no air bubbles. Ensure that your chemicals are fully dissolved before coating paper or fabric.
Very dark with blue highlights.	– Overexposed. – If using a negative it could be that it wasn't opaque enough.	– If it's due to overexposure, keep an eye on light levels when working outside. Remember prints continue to darken as they dry. – It's possible to lightly bleach an overexposed print using a very dilute solution of sodium carbonate (washing soda). – If it's because of an overly transparent negative, printing the same image onto acetate or contact-negative film twice then very carefully taping them together can make a more opaque negative.
Big white areas spoiling an otherwise nice print, or a pale washed-out print you're tempted to put in the bin.	– Depends on your design. – One of the first three issues, listed opposite.	Re-coat the paper and print again. This can add interest when a print is unbalanced by big leaf shapes for example. Overprinting/double-exposure is always fun and worth doing deliberately.

Reusing and recycling your scraps

It's almost always worth trying to recoat and overprint a pale result, but if you really don't want to keep a print or you like only a section of it, you might find that you have lots of left-over fragments and scraps of paper or fabric after all your printing. For every image I choose to stitch into and frame, there are several sulking in a drawer because they didn't make the cut. I have boxes full of interesting off-cuts that I can't bear to throw away, as doing so feels wasteful.

It's an irony that many creative practices involve quite a lot of consumption – often with expensive materials – yet we as creatives are typically very sensitive to these issues. However, there are things we can do to make a tiny difference.

A very meta example was a lovely print studio I taught at where they used the 'misprints' from my cyanotype workshop in a paper-making workshop the following week, and then printed again on the 'new' paper!

My favourite use for unloved prints is to die-cut labels and collage shapes using my little die-cutting machine; this works well with fabric too.

Fabric scraps can be twisted into twine if you have the patience (see left – I've got quite addicted to this as a way to feel busy while my mind wanders!), and larger pieces can be sewn together to use for crazy quilting or for small fabric collage projects (see the top of page 20).

However, because I don't want to encourage the hoarding many artists and makers are prone to ('...but it might come in handy one day'), and because all the fabrics and paper are made from natural fibres, they can all go safely into a compost heap or recycling bin, leaving a lovely clear workspace to start all over again for new cyanotype adventures!

LAST WORD

Finally, because it would be sad to end with a section on mistakes and compost heaps...

I hope your interest in cyanotype has been ignited, and you've gained enough confidence in the process to keep on playing and learning. You will probably have started looking at everything a bit differently, noticing plants that have interesting silhouettes, hoping the sun will be at the right angle when you get home from work, or wondering if your pet would stay still long enough for you to catch their shadow...

Cyanotype printing seems so closely linked with nature and the elements, and is the perfect way to celebrate them.

I admit I've sometimes had a love-hate relationship with cyanotype over the course of writing this book, but ultimately the love has won because I'm still learning: I definitely want to do more with plant tannin toning and I plan to collect lots more alder cones, oak galls and other plant material next autumn. It still feels magical when the image appears during rinsing, and I still dream of having the sewing skills to make a bamboo silk dress with a cotton velvet coat all printed with swallows and cow parsley and spring sunshine...

Have fun! x

TEMPLATES

All of the templates on these pages are provided at 100% scale, and can be scanned or traced off as is. The Hare template, below, and the Topiary Garden Pop-up Card template opposite, are for personal use only; please do not sell any items using these templates.

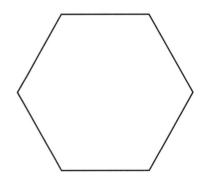

Downloadable templates

These templates are also available to download free from the Bookmarked Hub website:

www.bookmarkedhub.com

Search for this book by title or ISBN: the files can be found under 'Book Extras'.

Membership of the Bookmarked online community is free.

Hare
Fabric Night Lights project,
pages 78–85

Hexagon
'Patchwork' Tote Bag project,
pages 72–77

©witchmountain

APPENDIX

Glossary

Alt. process
Short for 'alternative photographic process' –
usually hand-made, photographic printing
processes, often made without a camera.

Contact print
Like a photogram, this describes a print made
by laying an object or negative directly onto
the prepared paper.

D-max
Maximum density. This refers to the darkest
blue in a print.

Edition
A number of prints made from one plate or
negative, which then form a limited collection.

Exposure
The length of time a print is left in the light
to produce an image.

Oxidization
The process whereby the iron salts change
colour with exposure to light and oxygen to
make Prussian blue.

pH
The scale measuring acidity to alkalinity, with
'neutral' being pH7.

Photogram
Making a print by laying actual objects onto
light-sensitive paper.

Suppliers

Firstcall Photographic
Jacquard cyanotype chemicals, light-proof bags
and papers.
www.firstcall-photographic.co.uk

Heaton Cooper Studio
Khadi papers, book and card blanks, watercolour
paper and other lovely art materials. It's also my
local art shop, who also happen to have a great
online store.
www.heatoncooper.co.uk

Cyanotype UK
UV light units, acetate, contact-negative film, kits
and tutorials.
www.cyanotype.co.uk

Hobbycraft
General craft supplies including brushes, embroidery
hoops and air-dry clay.
www.hobbycraft.co.uk

Organic Textile Company
Natural fabrics and fabric blanks for printing.
www.organiccotton.biz

Dannells®
Lampshade-making kits
www.dannells.com

Further reading

FOR ADULTS

Alternative Photography
Website covering all forms of 'alt. process'.
www.alternativephotography.com

Christina Z. Anderson
Photographer, teacher and writer. Her books offer a really in-depth study of the science behind cyanotype, which will be of particular interest to photographers. There is also a volume on image toning using plant materials.
www.christinazanderson.com

Cyanutopia
A fascinating podcast hosted by Marolyn Krasner about all things cyanotype.
www.marolynkrasner.com

Mike Ware
Writings on the science, history and practical applications of all forms of 'alt. process', including free downloads, UK and international links and suppliers.
www.mikeware.co.uk

Cyanotypes on Fabric: A blueprint on how to produce ... blueprints!
By Ruth Brown; self-published in 2016.
ISBN-13: 978-09-5546-475-1
This is a very useful book if you're interested in cyanotype printing on fabric.

World Cyanotype Day
A website and social media group celebrating cyanotype on the last Saturday in September.
www.worldcyanotypeday.com

FOR CHILDREN

The Bluest of Blues
By Fiona Robinson; published by Abrams in 2019.
ISBN-13: 978-1-41972-551-7
A beautiful picture book telling the story of Anna Atkins.

Sunprint paper
Widely available pre-coated, light-sensitive paper.
www.sunprints.org

Endnotes

PAGE 8

From an article by Johnny McAwley on the Slightly Blue website:
<https://shorturl.at/euOZ0>

PAGE 9

TOP PHOTOGRAPH
This blueprint is dated 1887, and was the design for a new paper machine supplied by Bertram's of Edinburgh after a disastrous fire destroyed Burneside Mill in 1886. Featured with kind permission from, and remains the copyright of, James Cropper PLC. For more information about the company, please visit the website: www.jamescropper.com

MIDDLE PHOTOGRAPH
'Sir John Herschel'
Artist: Julia Margaret Cameron (1815–1879)
Date: 1867
Collection: Gilman Collection, Purchase, Robert Rosenkranz Gift, 2005
Source: The Met Collection, via the Metropolitan Museum of Art, New York

BOTTOM PHOTOGRAPH
'Portrait of Anna Atkins'
Artist: unknown
Date: ca. 1862
Collection: Nurstead Court Archives
Source: Nurstead Court Archives

PAGE 11

TOP-LEFT PHOTOGRAPH
Title page in Part I of *Photographs of British Algae: Cyanotype Impressions*
Artist/author: Anna Atkins
Date: 1845–1853
Collection: Gilman Collection, Purchase, The Horace W. Goldsmith Foundation Gift, through Joyce and Robert Menschel, 2005
Source: The Met Collection, via the Metropolitan Museum of Art, New York

TOP-RIGHT PHOTOGRAPH
Introduction in Part I of *Photographs of British Algae: Cyanotype Impressions*
Artist/author: Anna Atkins
Date: 1845–1853
Collection: Spencer Collection, via John Herschel-Shorland
Source: New York Public Library Digital Collections

BOTTOM-LEFT PHOTOGRAPH
Rhodomenia laciniata in Part IV of *Photographs of British Algae: Cyanotype Impressions*
Artist/author: Anna Atkins
Date: 1845–1853
Collection: Spencer Collection, via John Herschel-Shorland
Source: New York Public Library Digital Collections

BOTTOM-RIGHT PHOTOGRAPH
Ptilota sericea in Part I of *Photographs of British Algae: Cyanotype Impressions*
Artist/author: Anna Atkins
Date: 1845–1853
Collection: Spencer Collection, via John Herschel-Shorland
Source: New York Public Library Digital Collections

PAGE 23

TOP PHOTOGRAPH
Copyright of Manuel Limay Incil, with kind permission. (www.instagram.com/manuel_limay_incil_fotografia/)

MIDDLE PHOTOGRAPH
Copyright of Jo Howell, with kind permission.
Jo Howell, via <https://shorturl.at/iqrM8>
(www.maverickbeyond.com)

PAGE 26

The record-breaking event can be found on the Guinness World Records website, here: <https://shorturl.at/inrvV>

INDEX

THANKS

I'd like to thank the people at Search Press for commissioning this project, particularly Emily and Maz whose expertise, hard work and enthusiasm turned my waffly Word document into something that looks like a real book!

Huge thanks to photographers Mark and Stacy, who worked their magic to capture the process and style the finished projects.

I'm grateful to the suppliers who gave me samples of their products to use. Many thanks to other cyanotype artists who have shared techniques and generously allowed me to use their images here.

'Imposter syndrome' is real, and I will always be indebted to my friends and wonderful family for listening to my constant doubts and totally dismissing them! I love you all more than toast and Marmite and cinnamon buns.

Finally, a special thank you to the Ko-fi supporters, especially Louis, Sue and Christyne, whose small but enormously kind donations helped more than you will ever know – and not just financially.

P.S. Thank you to you too, dear reader, for reading this far and buying this book x